LIVE YOUR
YOUNIQUE
LIFE

Becoming Your Authentic Self
So You Can Fulfill Your Unique
Purpose

JOY ISEKI

To all the younique souls who have made the decision to live their authentic lives and be who they are without feeling inadequate.

This page is intentionally left blank.

PRAISE FOR LIVE YOUR YOUNIQUE LIFE

Your greatest obligation to yourself and the sphere of human existence is the alignment of your navigation within the earth school to how and for what you are wired. This is Joy Iseki's call to you.

Joseph ITIAT
Spiritual Evolutionist

Live Your Younique Life is a book like no other. A mirror into one's very soul. If you are lost you will surely find your true self in it. It is not motivation based on hype but one that generates an intrinsic motivation from within you that can keep you going for a life time!

BATIFE Pereemiwei Solomon
Author, Political Maverick, Educationist and Entrepreneur

It was E.E. Cummings that wittily quipped, "To be nobody but yourself in a world that tries to make you everybody else means to fight the hardest battle and never stop fighting." He was right and Ms Joy Iseki, with her blockbuster book, shares timely and timeless principles that will help any and every individual who wants to achieve limitless success in the game of life. She demystified the myth that purpose is really not anywhere but in the heart of man, which can simply be discovered by embracing your authentic self. Ms Joy Iseki displays her gift as a creative and a courant writer when she opined, "To find your true-north, that is, your true-self, you will need to embrace authenticity as a means to discovering your life's greatest purpose. The iron-lady herself poured all her heart into creating this gem of a book and I will herein recommend it for individuals who are tired of the status quo, tired of being normal and tired of being just-an-average-Joe to becoming extraordinary and highly successful individuals who will turn the world upside down.

Orator Samuel ADEYINKA

Accelerate Income Mastermind, Lagos Nigeria

I have read your book. I commend you for your ideas, passion and purpose. The subject of focus is important for this generation of Nigerians and all those who want to make a difference. Keep it up.

Chizor Wisdom DIKE

President, Development Needs and Research Services

Portharcourt, Nigeria

The perfect comparison to life is a movie. Roles in a movie are uniquely different from one actor to another so as to achieve the ultimate aim of the producer, therefore a unique script is written to suit these roles. Can you, therefore, imagine what will happen to an actor that refuses to follow a prepared script for his role? He would be disgraced and replaced. Reputation damaged. Future unsecured. Therefore, actors don't envy other actors' roles. Actors don't copy other actors' roles. Actors don't compare their roles. They just go on stage to act their unique roles to the best of their abilities.

Joy Iseki, in this beautiful gift to the world, *Live Your Younique Life* beams light to our lives like a movie, so as to reveal in simple and concise manner, why and how to stick to our individual unique scripts of life. What a well thought out book and very timely too!

Tomiwa OGUNREMI

Writer and Clarity Coach

www.tomiwaogunremi.com

CONTENTS

This page is intentionally left blank.

WHY THIS BOOK?

"If you judge a fish by its ability to climb a tree, it will live its whole life believing that it is stupid."
ALBERT EINSTEIN

You are a different soul. Your life is absolutely designed by the Creator to suit your uniqueness. Everything about you is for that purpose. And quite naturally, you lived and accepted it that way in your childhood until you started to "grow up" into what the environment expected that you should be. And then also began your confusion about your purpose, something that was never missing in the place of your authenticity.

Being different is not what most of us have been brought up to be. In fact, it's like the one thing we were taught, subtly, not to dare become, especially here in our part of the world. Everything about our culture makes this very clear. You are expected to behave as they have always done. You are not expected to ask why. Hence, the day one shows whether by example or in words that they are choosing a different path, that day may be the last day of their "good old" days. Doing that gets you labelled as rebellious.

Consequently, most people have grown up as zombies. That is not how it should be. Deprived of the ability to be authentic, most of us have grown up to be clueless as to who we are, simply drifting in the direction of the trend or things we have seen overtime in society.

The impact of this approach is huge, and that, negatively. As a country, we are not inventing because children are robbed of the chance to deploy themselves within the parameters of how they are built. As individuals, most of have no idea what it feels like to live the life we are built for, day to day. Authenticity calls forth originality. It calls for a uniquely creative lifestyle.

Nothing else suits better than being your authentic self. Your purpose, creativity and fulfilment are connected to this. You are the one to create your narrative, and that can only happen if you choose to be intentional in your choices. Failing to be intentional in the choices you make might mean choosing a path that does not lead to a better knowledge of yourself. And that, can lead to someone else putting you to use.

The liberating truth is, your uniqueness matters in the final equation, and forms the premise for which this book is written. This book is designed to call forth the uniqueness in you. It is designed to awaken you to live your life.

Here then, is your chance to live your younique life!

Joy Iseki
October 01, 2017

BEING AUTHENTIC: WHAT IT MEANS

"Are you doing what you love? Are you telling the people that matter how much you love and appreciate them on a regular basis? Are you being true to yourself in your thoughts and actions?"

ANONYMOUS

I am pretty much an extrovert, although prone to an extreme introspection, especially when I am on my creative side. For many years, I struggled with being me. I wished and cried for the freedom to just be myself. I did not mind erring on the side of perfection rather than being an all-pure version of what I could never sustain, of what I was not.

I was different. I knew that and it was like something everyone else knew too. But I never understood why I was so different. And no one seemed to have known why. While this was my reality, I was surrounded by expectations. I was expected to fit in, to live like others.

My attempt to do differently, or say, be myself, was not welcomed by a lot of people. This happens to be the same for most people and living within such atmosphere can be a difficult mountain to climb.

Life can be tough when you find yourself trying to live up to the expectations of everyone else except yourself. It can also feel very lonely trying to be yourself in a world where everyone else wants to be the same, a world where many people believe that the majority are always right.

Sadly, that is not true. Many beliefs and things we hold as norms are not always right. This is even truer in the context of people being expected to simply conform to the lifestyle around them, instead of take a stand for themselves.

You are uniquely created to live uniquely. To seek popular vote therefore is heading towards ending up like the rest of the people. No one knows satisfaction from living that way. There is so much internal misery in conforming to others at the expense of being authentic.

The decision to be lead authentic lives, while allowing others to live theirs is what should be common to everyone. That is because it can be a strong and beneficial guide for everyone. It can make you live your life on purpose and in definitive terms. It can make you see challenges as blessings in disguise.

Such is the result that can come from embracing the call to leading a younique life, a life of authenticity. While here, it is in your place to understand that you are ever-evolving and can only grow if you embrace authenticity, find your true self, live on purpose, while all along respecting the right of others to do same.

We are all created different and unique. We are peculiar beings, whether of the same race or of one family; we are different. Our uniqueness is actually the reason life can be so beautiful.

Life looses this beauty when we ignore the call to be authentic. Internal frustration is stimulated where multiple people strive to be like one another.

The world is better served, and we benefit better from each other by accepting the uniqueness in ourselves and from others. Through this do we attain balance as each of us gets to truly live life and fulfill purpose.

WHAT DOES AUTHENTICITY MEAN?

According to Wikipedia, "Authenticity is the degree to which one is true to one's own personality, spirit, or character, despite external pressures; the conscious self is seen as coming to terms with being in a material world and with encountering external forces, pressures, and influences which are very different from, and other than, itself". In other words, to be authentic is to understand that you are not the space you find yourself; it is staying original and choosing to behave and relate with others in ways that has no room for self-shaming.

Authenticity is the quality of being genuine or true. It is allowing yourself evolve without taking the form of another person's way of life. It means to be real and genuine, not a copy. To put it simply, it is the degree to which you are true to your traits and the acceptance of your peculiar personality.

Being authentic is being in your natural habitat. It shows in the way you talk, eat, speak, and think. Copying others should not be given consideration at all. Copying others is more expensive, relative to being yourself.

Being yourself is the effortless call that leads to bliss and expresses your uniqueness in all of creation. This has nothing to do with being perfect as some people assume. That happens to be the fear of some people.

They fear that they may sound too good to be true, and may be viewed with cynicism by others. They fear they may not be able to sustain living in their natural habitat. They think it is a call to being perfect, to being flawless. Hence, they choose to blend in.

Authentic is how we were when we entered the world. It is who you were naturally before the interferences of other factors such as the knowledge of your race, schools, environment and all kinds of nurture. It is who your heart knows as being your true self.

Authenticity is a call into your natural self. It is simply asking you to be real with yourself and about yourself. And that realness is in your heart and bears witness with who you are becoming.

If your personality is not in congruence with your heart, you will know by virtue of the lack of peace in your life. And if you lack this peace with self, you will not experience the peace outside too because your inner peace is what makes peace between you and the outside world.

The truth is, being your true self is important to your entire wellbeing. It affects relationships, business, and all tiers of life. Once you are living your authentic life, it brings you the peace that translates into all of these other parts that make your whole.

AUTHENTICITY AND YOUR CREATIVITY

If you believe that you have been created by God and in His own image, then you should know that God as a Creator only birthed creative beings in order to continue the process of creation. Being one of His kind should make you expressive of this creative provision. Recognition of this reality is one of the keys to leading your younique life.

Realness is spontaneous. Hence, authenticity is connected with creativity. You are never acting out every time you express who you are. And that is what makes you unique. Your first duty to yourself is to accept that you are a uniquely created individual, not only deserving to be heard and known, but equipped for that.

You deserve to express who you are in a world where copycatting seems the way of life. In other words, if anyone is to live the life of another person, do not let it be you. Those who want to be somebody else do so because they feel inadequate about themselves. One reason for that is because of the narratives they've been given.

Whereas others may fake their lives, you should not. Instead of blend in, or copy others, you should choose to make the decision of rewriting whatever limiting and Self-denying script you have been given. It is in your place and power to create the life that suits your true identity.

That is what being authentic means. Of course, it requires a lot of willpower, as there is a raging war that threatens our identity. The call for conformity is high. We are made to believe that we have to behave like some other groups of people before we can be accepted or even belong. And so we lose ourselves to this idea of being like everyone else. We literally lose ourselves subtly without being aware of it.

No one lacks in will or power. The requirement is putting the two together. You must be on your toes therefore and alert over what concerns your life. This must be so because you cannot afford to be the duplicate of someone else's life. You cannot afford to lose you while you are still alive.

Losing your realness is actually a death to everything else you'd have become. Spontaneity arises mostly from being natural, from not having to rehearse to be. That is how it feels to be your real self. And it is the reason it can unlock your creative ability, more especially since you do not have to exert so much stress on your mind when functioning in your place of design.

That is not the experience when trying to copy someone else. The display of creativity in many of our entertainers and superstars are due to their originality. That is why they became superstars in the first place. They are not among the "common" crowd because they have embraced themselves and believed in their unique abilities.

Interestingly, we are all superstars! To shine however, you have to be your own unique star. You have to dare to be yourself first of all. It may look difficult to choose a different path, especially one not so popular like living to become your true self. It can look and even be daunting to start on that path, but in the end, it holds a far more reward than anything you would have copied.

To not spend your last days on earth wishing you could get another chance to re-live life, make use of this chance to live the life you are created for. Choosing to stay true to yourself over blending in is being authentic.

REFLECTIONS

On a personal ground, what would you say being authentic means?

_____

_____

_____

_____

_____

_____

_____

_____

How would you differentiate the call to authenticity from the paradigm of perfection?

_____

_____

_____

_____

_____

_____

_____

_____

How would you describe the correlation of authenticity to the experience of peace and the deployment of your creative part?

_____

_____

_____

_____

_____

_____

AUTHENTICITY AND YOUR LIFE PURPOSE

"I can be a better me than anyone can."
DIANA ROSS

When I was much younger, I loved the idea of buying and selling. I also loved taking the lead in talk sessions. I enjoyed brainstorming sessions and engaging in philosophical reasoning. In the early nineties, while still in Primary Two, a particular experience stands out.

Living with my parents in Ikeja, there was a church close to my house that was always holding various programmes. From time to time, I would watch them from our balcony. When I do this, I would see their members walk around during break sessions. Then one day, while still watching from our balcony, a business idea struck.

It occurred to me that some of their members were probably thirsty, hence would patronize me if I sold cold water to them. We had a very good refrigerator that could cool liquids really fast. Right there, I saw a business opportunity.

Swiftly, I checked the house for some sachet nylon which we used to call "Santana" nylon at the time. I got those sachet nylons, got some bottled water out of our freezer and began to fill them up with water. Pouring about a medium cup quantity into each nylon, I would end up with quite some numbers in my basket!

I would then go to the entrance of the church where other vendors were situated, to sell my product to the church members. I would sell out my product and keep running back and forth to the house for refill. I was about eight years old at the time.

Though excited at how much money I was making, I refused to stop there. Having money in my hands meant I could do some other things. It meant I could try something innovative. This was just about the time when the popular colouring candy "Balewa" was in the market and being improvised as local ice cream. Kids loved the sweetness.

I decided to go buy this "Balewa" and do the same thing I had done with my water business. "Balewa" was the name we called the colorant that melted upon dissolution in water. When poured and tied in one of those "Satana" nylons in its liquid state, it solidifies and becomes blocked in a freezer. Kids would lick it from the nylon through a cut out hole like an ice cream. I am not sure we still have those around now. They were like candy that coloured the tongue and teeth while being licked. And we just loved them back then growing up.

I would buy some of this balewa candies, melt them in ice cold water, add some bits of sugar, have them filled in those "Satana" sachet, then keep them refrigerated till blocked. Turned out, I sold those stuff like hot cake!

Enjoying myself, I did this "business" for weeks before my dad reprimanded me on the use of our fridge for business purposes. This was something that should have been considered a huge signal by my parents.

Whereas I should have been encouraged, I was warned instead. I had to obey; I had to live up to the expectations of my dad. It was his refrigerator after all. I was disappointed that using the refrigerator to serve the family was given precedence over a nudge at purpose.

YOUR PURPOSE IS IN YOUR HEART

Growing up without a clear guide on the concept of authenticity, let alone purpose, I have had to strive to figure out what way to go on my own. Over the years, I have attended seminars and conferences that focused on finding purpose.

I came to love those speakers as they made great impression on me. They were, to me, living their purpose and maximizing their full potentials. I wished earnestly to be like them since I also wanted to feel fulfilled. Some of them warned me about how not living the purpose for which I was created for would mean I could not fully live my life. I read books saying similar things. But things were not the same for me.

I was feeling frustrated, filled with fear of not fully maximizing my life because I just couldn't grasp my purpose as I was being taught.

That was a difficult period for me. Desperate to figure this out, I searched even further, outside me, for what I was created for. I found out with time that I was not alone in this dilemma; many people were in my shoes, especially those who, like me, were determined to live on purpose. However, I was determined to solve the puzzle. The search continued, but it led me to a different conclusion.

There is a correlation between authenticity and purpose. That makes it a huge error to try to be like someone else. This attempt is always a deviation from the path that can give clarity on what one is built for. Aside from being a deviation, it slows down the speed at which one can find answers to the question of what one's life is planted on earth for.

Coming to the place of truth becomes a high need. Truth sets free. When this occurs, there is always a knowing. My search for my life's purpose brought me to that conclusion. In my search, I found something that changed my life forever. I realized that our purpose is in our hearts.

That is the liberating truth. Your purpose is in your heart. It was set in there by God. King Solomon captured this well when he said, "He has also set eternity in the human hearts." In other words, God has set in your heart what you have been designed to be even before the foundation of the world. Towing a similar vein, King Solomon again said, "Whatever is has already been and what will be has been before." In other words, what you are designed to be is not a sudden development. The world only awaits your materialization.

This materialization cannot happen unless the path of authentic living is embraced. In other words, without paying attention to what your tendencies are, you cannot have a glimpse of what your calling might be.

As adults, having been schooled by those who have no clue as to why we are here, we struggle with this. That explains why purpose is freely evident when we are children. We always seem clear, and excited, until we start being affected by the interferences of life itself.

There, begins, mostly, our struggle.

When I delved into business as a kid and experienced a boom, I felt so good. But no one discussed that with me. Whereas I could venture into commerce and make money at such a young age, it was not lauded or considered a sign of entrepreneurial tendency, but mere digress from what was more important – "schooling".

Whereas that was my family's chance to tutor and get me properly schooled, prepped for greater clarity, and pushed in the direction my tendency, I was not offered that. I was offered resistance instead. I resisted for a while, refused to be stopped completely, and kept doing little side businesses, even up to my second year in secondary school. But they had won somehow.

Their consistent resistance had created a compounded effect on me, and brought me to submission to what was a norm. I had started feeling ashamed of what I was doing. I did not look normal, did not look like what was the common practice, and hence, I got conditioned to live as others. I joined the rat race.

I had to read to pass like every kid. I had to think that the way out is to get good grades, divorce entrepreneurship from my thinking, and allow myself to be prepped, not for commerce, but for job-hunting.

For many people, this story resonates.

There are many people who are doing things that they are not built for. In some cases, they know this, but having bought into survival thinking and conditioned to live like others, they have not been able to deploy their will in taking the path that leads to their authentic nature.

These, though making money in some cases, do not know fulfilment. Fulfilment in life is dependent on doing what you are built for. It is obtained from operating in your natural habitat. Whereas it may not give you lots of monetary returns, and can, if harnessed in tandem with the right enablers, the satisfaction that being in your habitat generates is far greater than monetary returns.

Your dominant tendencies, when not powered by the opinion of others, is a huge sign of what path you should walk. The call on all humans is to find this blueprint, and walk in the direction of same design. We are not here to do the thinking of others, and even good intentions are no reasons to compromise on being you.

Purpose, why you are here, is resident within the landscape of how you are wired. And this knowledge, this push, is resident in your heart. The truth is, authenticity and purpose are a twin, and you need both to steer your course in the space of humanity.

As teenagers, my friends and I, just after the completion of our high school education, learnt about how drug abuse was becoming a serious issue among students. Driven by the desire to provide leadership, in this case, see more students focused on their personal development, we would go to a popular public school in Oregun where we lived, on a regular basis and address students in regard to this.

At the core of our being, we wanted to see healthy and sensible teenagers. We were teenagers, no doubt, but the push from within, was to make a difference by reaching out. All we had in our possession was the passion to make impact and change the mindset of these students toward illicit drug use.

All that mattered to us was making a difference. That drive made us unstoppable. At one point, we went soliciting for funds to hold a seminar for the senior class students of the school at the major event centre, then in Oregun. We had huge turnout for the seminar and the project was successful.

The thrill, the joy, the happiness we felt was beyond words. It was unquantifiable. It was done for free, but it gave us lots of fulfilment. It was a huge indicator of what we were born to do. You should not ignore the things you do for free that leave you feeling fulfilled despite not being paid. Even that, can act as an indicator to your life's purpose.

Though knowing several thrills at several points where I was myself, I had taken in so much of what society had sold me. It had affected me to the extent I could not readily step out of the crowd anymore. Consequently, I struggled with what to do with my life at some point.

I remember sending out so many CVs after graduation from the University. I did all sort of things in my bid for a white collar offer but never got one and could not think of what business to do. I had already blended, though not without internal struggles. I had lived, trying to fit in with the rest of the crowd.

For almost six years of my life, as an adult, I virtually struggled with even the jobs I was able to finally secure. My heart cried out for more from me. I was too afraid of the decisions I had to make. In the end, I had to do what was honourable. I had to choose the path of authentic living. I resigned my job. By this time, I was already an award-winning staff. But I had to go. I knew it was time to follow my heart cry. And like those who have had to follow their heart cry, I have no regrets.

A pay check is good. There is a place for that. But there is no honour in living for a pay check so you can simply get by when you can be more and know fulfilment. There is no honour in blending with the crowd when you are supposed to stand out. While you may not have to resign your job, and should not do so without a clear plan, you should take the path of the authentic aspirations of your heart.

As a human being, your first duty to self is to identify what makes you different. How you are different from others can offer insight into how you should conduct your affairs. Authenticity is the only way you can live on purpose. It is the only way you can make informed decisions. If I had the hindsight to look into my childhood, or more into my heart, I would have started what I am presently doing much earlier.

We all have our purpose boldly there in our hearts. If we are introspective enough and sincere with Self, we would not be in a long search, struggling to find out our life's purpose. This struggle, among other reasons, is because we lost our sense of authenticity at childhood.

To find that true north now, we may have to go back to that childhood. That, for me, can be the game changer. Aside that, I have found out that the key to finding purpose is to embrace the call to authenticity.

To lead your life in ways that lead to useful discovery, you must walk the path of authenticity. It takes the confidence to be yourself to find yourself. That means, until there is the willingness to pay attention to your tendencies, and that, confidently, you can rarely establish clearly, what your purpose is.

Life is not linear at all as many would love it to be. Nothing great happens in a straight, predictable way. There are always chances for some occurrences that create curves. However, when we are in our natural state, we flow with ease and can in that direction, live on purpose. You can, in the bid to make meaning of the curves you meet, dealing with these issues in authentic ways, discover your true self, and know clearly, the aspirations of your heart.

I have had to learn this through the processes life has brought me through. Your purpose, you will realize, is the most natural thing to you. And that is in you already, in your heart. You only need to allow it flow out.

Letting it flow out must be done through deliberate effort, through knowledge that comes through self-awareness. This clarity happens when your conclusions are made in alignment with those predominant desires in your heart.

This means you must as a matter jealousy, resist society, cultural and environmental restrictions and tendencies from conditioning you to believe otherwise. In other words, you should not allow others to tutor you on how you are "supposed" to be.

The confusion lies in telling people to find purpose. For many, this leads to a search in futility. If this is not fully grasped, people would keep going around in circles. Liberation and direction lies in becoming a little child again. Paraphrasing the words of Jesus Christ, become like one of these little ones so you can access the kingdom that is within you.

Those who are fortunate to have guardians in possession of this understanding are guided accordingly. Those without this are mostly confused. And there be many who are stuck in what they do not like.

You do not need to like everything you find yourself doing. But even that, is useful information. Whenever someone comes to me confused and perplexed about life, wondering if what they are presently doing fits into their purpose, I tell them, "Whatever you find to do, do it well."

The key is to embrace everything with an open mind, with the way you are wired. That way, you will get the right feedback as to whether you are in your purpose or not. You cannot do this if you live as a copy cat, hence the need to stay authentic and not just follow people.

In embracing whatever you do with the right attitude, you get useful information. You learn along the way what it is you should or should not be doing.

Authenticity is related to purpose. It is the expression of your true self in congruence with how you think, feel and act. Though part of what we have lost to being adult, it is not beyond the reach of anyone. All it takes is paying attention to yourself, asking yourself honest questions, providing yourself honest answers and becoming more self-aware.

In knowing how you are, you can tell what moves you and what does not. In knowing what moves you and what does not move you, you can tell what direction to go. Authenticity and purpose are a twin that can make you live your younique life.

REFLECTIONS

What would you say are the aspirations of your heart?

_____

_____

_____

_____

_____

_____

_____

_____

To stay on the path of your purpose, what are the things you would have to do?

_____

_____

_____

_____

_____

_____

_____

Beginning with the end in mind, write down what you hope to have achieved at the end of your time on planet Earth?

_____

_____

_____

_____

_____

_____

_____

WHY YOU SHOULD BE YOUNIQUE

"The more you like yourself, the less you are like anyone else, which makes you unique"
WALT DISNEY

For the purpose of this book, let me clarify what being younique means. I coined it from two words, "you" and "unique". We know that unique is also a synonym for different. To be unique is to be different or original and not a copy, and "you" is used as the subject of a verb which in this case, is you! So for the purpose of this discourse, to be younique is to be your unique self.

Naturally, you are different. Your fingerprint confirms this. Not even identical twins are in possession of identical fingerprints. This fact, that your fingerprint is not the same with any of the billions of humans on earth is a huge indication that you are not built to be like anyone.

You should not be afraid of being yourself therefore, and you should not waste the precious opportunity to be part of the human race, trying to be like anyone.

Living your younique life is therefore a call upon you to embrace your difference and live your life. It is, has always, and will always be rewarding. It does require firmness on your path, and might lead to all kinds of opposition from even those close to you, but its gain outweighs whatever pain you might go through. Among others, there are four benefits of living your younique life.

IT BRINGS FREEDOM

There is so much we gain from being our natural self. And one that we cannot deny is being free. Being yourself gives you freedom. You no longer have to work yourself out trying to please anyone or learning to be someone else. That gives you focus and makes you stand out.

Being yourself frees you from that urge to always want to live up to only what others want of you even if it meant that you had to sometimes do this against your own will and values. Many have become hypocrites for fear of whether they would still be loved should they express what is in their heart.

In living your younique life, you grow beyond becoming a prisoner of other people's expectations. You live as a truly free being, able to help others experience freedom as well. Interestingly, you cannot truly help others live a good life you have not experienced yourself.

That's the core of authenticity; you first of all find yourself, build up yourself and love yourself while fulfilling purpose. Then with this experience and capacity, you help build others up.

This idea of self-love is in the true definition of love, which is that you love your neighbour as yourself! But if you haven't loved self, how then do you love your neighbour as yourself? No one gives what they do not have.

You cannot give what you don't have. If you haven't placed value on yourself, there will be no way you can appreciate value in others or even give them value.

True freedom is in you knowing that you are living the life you have been born to live. It is you having the right to be yourself with anyone you find yourself without being ashamed or having the urge to be pleasing to them against your heart's leading.

It does not suggest selfishness or disregard for other people's feelings and beliefs. However, you will have to master where to place that balance.

This freedom, obtained from living your younique life, always have the heart as its first witness. You will know when it occurs because of the inner peace it brings with it.

IT HELPS YOU LIVE ABOVE SHAME

If anyone was ever so ashamed of who they were, I must have been the one. It wasn't just about being shy, it was also about being ashamed of everything about myself. For the worst part, I wasn't even aware of how much this was affecting my self-esteem. Neither did I understand why I felt ashamed about self.

When I became more aware, I realized the role my thoughts played. From wrong and disempowering thoughts, I became a victim of my own life gradually. You see, our thoughts have a way of playing out on us if we are not intentional about it. My personal growth then was at a minus level because I had no confidence to start anything.

Accepting myself for who I am became the starting point for me. Beyond that, I also learnt to give thanks for who I am. I had to change the game by being grateful one by one for those things my mind was using against me. I started being grateful that I had so many things working well for me, I was grateful that I could read and assimilate really fast. I was grateful for strength and a great health. I made gratitude a habit.

The idea was to concentrate on what I had working for me so I could build up my self-image first. You cannot imagine how this slow but formative process started to work on my mind and the result was transformational. Not only did I come out of it, I started seeing the good sides of the things I had felt ashamed of.

True change starts from the mind. Our thoughts are what our lives become. Being at your authentic state could make you more comfortable with self. It's like being in your own skin and still comfortable in it. The feeling of shame could be because of some self-judgment which may have been as a result of guilt, sadness, something you might have done wrong or an awkward moment of embarrassment.

People who have come to terms with their real selves rarely feel ashamed. This is because they have mastered the act of accepting themselves, laughing even at themselves, so there's nothing left for anyone to mock them over. They key concept here is that they have come to accept who they are, regardless. I think Lao Tzu said it well when he said concerning self-acceptance that, "Because one believes in oneself, one doesn't try to convince others. Because one is content with oneself, one doesn't need others' approval. Because one accepts oneself, the whole world accepts him or her."

Self-acceptance then can help us overcome the approval we so much seek from others.

There are people who feel ashamed of their family background. Despising where you come from especially as regards the choice of your family, something that you had no control over is ridiculous and a disheartening reason to live a miserable life. No one ever had control over where their birth occurred. Interestingly, even that, what family we are born to, if properly received and harnessed, will enhance living an authentic life.

While one earth, no one should permit something as mere as a family background to limit their growth and chances of living to the fullest. You cannot let your background define you. You are actually who you have chosen to become regardless of where you may be coming from. You are who you have always been even before your birth on Earth. Somebody had to conceive you so you can be alive here on Earth, and that, for a purpose.

I feign no ignorance of some opportunities that may accrue to some people by reason of their birth. But that percentage is small compared to the larger masses. Ultimately, all of us do become who we are regardless of our birth place, even though it might seem easier for some people by birthright. But if you look around you, not all the famous people in the world for instance were born with silver spoons. That goes for most of the successful people we see.

Different things are responsible for the feeling of shame. However, what it is that we may have gone through or are not proud of, our embrace of authentic living can raise us above the grab of shame. There is no height you cannot attain. No dream too grand. Right from where you are now, with a simple will to be your younique self, you can take create the life you ought to have.

IT CAN BOOST YOUR SELF-CONFIDENCE

Confidence is the quality of being certain or a feeling or consciousness of one's powers. Self-confidence therefore has to do with how much certainty or believe you have in yourself. It is that trait that would make you stand without feeling self-condemned. It has nothing to do with your perfection. It only demonstrates a state of awareness.

Being yourself is a proof you have confidence in who you are and will therefore not act or copy anyone else. One of the core traits of authenticity is confidence. Until you commit to living your younique life, to being the person you are built to be, you won't attain consistency, which can lead to confidence in your ability to stay true to yourself without care for copycatting.

True confidence stems from an acceptance of self, from the understanding that you are different, and cannot aspire to be like anyone. Decide to commit to your true nature and fully accept yourself therefore. This gives the confidence to do other things, relate open-mindedly with other people, and have greater faith in your abilities. When we tow this path, it changes our outlook on things, and interpretation of even our past experiences, things we may have wished were not part of our history.

Growing up for me was not entirely rosy and I had a lot of reasons to hold back, to be laid back and to hold a poor view of myself. Confidence wasn't a word in my vocabulary. Having suffered shameful feelings, being confident was like a dread to me.

As you would agree, shame and lack of self-confidence usually go together because it would make you feel bad about yourself. But as I became more aware of who I was, I decided that I won't allow anything to hold me back from being the best I could possibly be.

The truth is, our seemingly disadvantaged past or present, those things that we are ashamed of in our lives hold for us an opportunity for greatness. In the absence of my struggles, I am not sure I would have discovered my authentic self. This is why I often say that everyone can lead the authentic life.

Everyone is inexcusable. Adversity may come, and seem to always do, but that should not be a reason to choose a low life. Instead of that, it should be confronted and used as a material for the creation of a better version of ourselves.

Your suffering should bring out only the best in you. Like diamonds, consider them your needful medium for personal transformation. And your authentic self is your best self. It is the only version of you that can confidently go through all that life will throw at you.

I read somewhere that authenticity can lead to better coping strategies, stronger sense of self-worth, more confidence, and a higher likelihood to following through on your goals. I totally agree with this. It is really a worthwhile mission then to do the best of all that you can, in order to be your authentic self.

An even more interesting thing about living your younique life is the fact that it takes you less effort to be yourself than it does trying to be who you are not. There is no point wishing to be somebody else, have someone else's eyes, or may be their heights and stuff like that.

Do not look at yourself and rarely notice what's good about you. At all times, understand that there are people wishing to be like you. Focus on understanding the entity called you, and create the life that you want to have.

As I learn more authentic living and how it breeds confidence, I have realized it is more about being daring by every little step you can take with what you know you have. I remember how I would volunteer to take up some roles in our local community Church gatherings. That was something I would not have done before, but could do from the moment I choose to be authentic. Sounds insignificant, but it was really huge considering how far away from being authentic I was.

Successful people start at the place of authenticity. They are those who have accepted their true self regardless of what they have been allotted by nature. And because they have accepted themselves, they become aware of what they have been allotted, and knowing that they have the power to create with all they have been given, they put themselves to use.

Most of them, though vulnerable like others, start with little acts of daring. Understand that you are not void of this power, the power to accept yourself and create the life you ought to have with what you have. To put it simply, you are not without the power to accept your originality and enjoy being a good, strong, yet flawed and vulnerable human being.

One thing about confidence that is spurred through authenticity is that it is not just spoken about, it is practiced. The practice is dependent on believing that you can stay in control of how your life turns out. This feeling of control comes from the practice of control. The practice of control will lead to competence in controlling your reception of what goes on in your life. This feeling of competence will lead to more feeling of confidence in yourself. All of these start at the place of making the commitment to live your younique life.

It was a long process for me because I was badly damaged after years of an identity struggle. Just as it was with me, you may be struggling in some way or may have been in my shoes before, irrespective of what the situation is, the key thing is you can and should live the life you have been built for.

On this planet you will meet people and situations that might want to threaten your position. You may meet with those who seem to possess better skills than you, and a feeling of unworthiness might arise. Dealing with such moments is easy when you have practiced authenticity and living your unique life. The confidence to snub such internal suggestions can only come from a good understanding of yourself, of the path you have walked, and of the fact that you are not the person standing next to you.

To fight this good fight of faith; to stick with what you believe is worth you having and experiencing in life; to not be easily moved or moved at all in your journey of life, you must delete the psychology of competition with others from your thinking completely.

This decision must be deliberate because left to chance, you will die a copy. No one fight cultural norms and limiting beliefs by chance. It is always done deliberately. Whatever strives to militate against your embrace of authentic living must become witness to your commitment to authentic living.

Whereas this battle will mostly be in your mind, you have to deal with it all the same. Of course people will throw their ways, belief systems and thinking at you, in attempt to get you to veer off the path you should walk. These too, you must resist.

The confidence to resist, to fight, to pull down what does not support purposeful living is found in the practice of authenticity, in the commitment to living your younique life. Your fight won't be in blows and blues, but in goodness and kindness; in the expression of who you are, what you believe and what you know the standard of your life should be.

This fight, which of course will cause your authentic self to evolve in the process, can only be sustained through the confidence that stems from living your younque life. Sheri L dew was quite apt when she said this of confidence, "Noble and great. Courageous and determined. Faithful and fearless. That is who you are and who you have always been. And understanding it can change your life, because this knowledge carries a confidence that cannot be duplicated any other way." Living the authentic life indeed breeds confidence.

IT POWERS PURPOSEFUL LIVING

Your purpose is already inside of you regardless of how far you might have travelled to go find it outside of yourself. When you fully embrace your unique self for all that it is, then like the child you once were, your heart begins to lead you to that call that had always been there before.

As mentioned earlier, your purpose is the most natural thing for you to do. It was never something you will have to be looking for in the first place. The disconnect was as a result of your "growing up", when you dropped all your heart desires at childhood to follow suit with the majority, to a way that seemed more like it to others who you gave the right to your life. This unfortunate thing happened because a unique soul attempted to live as a general being.

Authenticity will keep you on the right path and give you the right signal. You will stay within the frequency of living the life you are built for as long as you choose to pay attention to the nudges from your inner being. As long as you choose to copy no one, but be yourself, you will wake each day into better clarity of what you should be doing.

This should be the sole aspiration of every human being. No one should have any dream aside doing what they are created for, aside being the human being they are made to be.

It makes no sense to live on earth, acquire a lot, and pass on, just like most people, with all that you have been allotted. You should commit yourself to the sort of practices that empower for purposeful living. The embrace of authenticity, as a lifestyle, is one of such practices that powers purposeful living.

IT MAKES YOU A RECOGNIZABLE VOICE

Spiritual Evolutionist Joseph Itiat once said, "Strive to be one of the microscopic few who have cared enough to stay true to themselves, even at the expense of any form of societal correctness, doing only that which they strongly believe in, against the backdrop of their original configuration and allotted abilities, the extent to which they become easily recognizable, and have no need of repeated effort at self-introduction within their sphere of existence." Your aspiration, among other things, should be to lead a life that stands out, and is known for authenticity.

People should know you for who you are and what you represent, against the backdrop of your consistency in authentic conduct of your affairs. No one attains this consistency without the embrace of authenticity.

Living your younique life will make you stand out. It is a core trait of those who are committed to personal leadership. It is this attained distinction that guides even in the moment you may decide to be a voice to those without the ability to speak for themselves.

As one who deals with the struggles of life, and grows your person through walking the path of authenticity, you can easily relate with those who are themselves going through struggles. That means, you are eligible to offer help, to lend a hand.

This courage can only be found in living your younique life. You are rarely threatened, if at all, when you are an authentic person. Even in the moment you offer help, you do so freely, rarely feeling compelled.

This decision to be of help is not based on emotions, but on your ability to make controlled decisions. In other words, you are yourself at all times, owning your voice and doing only what you want. As a result, you are recognized and respected for that consistency in being you.

This approach to life has the potency of awakening the souls of others to living their younique life as well, for in seeing you, they see a model. For me, there is no greater contribution to the human sphere.

In helping others embrace authenticity through owning your voice and being a model, you create a stirring that leads to the manifestation of many sons and daughters of God. In other words, when people discover their authenticity, then they find it much easier to manifest what's in them and that in turn benefits other people. The beauty of life in finding the way things work and helping others do the same.

Living your real life makes you a voice indeed, as you lead other people to do same. This is especially important for those who still struggle with accepting their true selves. One should never hold back from others, lessons and experiences acquired in life. It is in sharing them that we bless. And being ourselves is a part of sharing our life with others.

That is in itself, a sort of storytelling that spurs to action.

REFLECTIONS

On what parameters would you think of yourself as living your younique life?

_____

_____

_____

_____

_____

If you haven't been living your younique life, what are things you would say are the reasons?

_____

_____

_____

_____

_____

Discuss freedom, confidence, and becoming a recognizable voice as offshoots of living your younique life?

_____

_____

_____

_____

_____

What steps will you take to improve on your competence so as to improve your confidence level?

_____

_____

_____

_____

_____

KNOWING YOU ARE BEING YOUNIQUE

*"We have to dare to be. If you let others tell you who you are,
you are living their reality — not yours."*
MAY SARTON

As human beings we can be very doubtful, both of ourselves, and other people. Once you have started this journey on authenticity, the next thing in your head might be doubts. You may begin to doubt yourself as to whether you are being real. And to some extent, this is good if it is done by way of self-check. Self-questioning of any kind can give useful information. By means of a checklist, it can assist you to gain clarity or even create balance.

Though mistaken by some to mean so, becoming younique is not becoming perfect, much less becoming holier than somebody else. That is quite different. Becoming you is simply accepting your uniqueness and choosing to live life that way. It is you choosing to go back to how you were at the beginning and giving an expression to your authentic self. It is steering true north. That is what fulfilling purpose is all about.

Everything that you are is already in your heart. You only need the courage to accept it and then begin to express it. This may not be void of doubt, but you won't be void of the push to express yourself as pertaining anything, the instant you align with your real self.

You become more open minded and not easily ashamed or embarrassed, even if that may mean being the only one with a different opinion. Accepting your youniquness makes you more open-minded. It makes you more receptive and willing to share yourself with others without fear of rejection or judgment.

I think there's something about being real that kind of makes you more human in a way that humanity should be made manifest. And part of that is not being so easily embarrassed about stuff because you are aware that you will make mistakes sometimes.

In accepting your humanity, you agree with the fact that irrespective of what you do, people will always form an opinion of you. In some cases, they will laugh at you. In other cases, they will talk about you. This knowledge helps in a way to make you more receptive of criticisms and so less ashamed of your errors, failures and mistakes.

Being you is the best thing you can offer to the world. It would make you easily more identifiable. And that's what we are looking for; people are tired of seeing the same thing, the same behaviour and the same way of life. The world craves souls that are bold enough to be truly real.

Your goal should be to be one of those who are true to themselves despite all the flaws and imperfections. These are easily known once seen. To know whether you are living your authentic life, let's look at what being authentic is not.

AUTHENTICITY IS NOT ABOUT BEING THE LOUDEST

There is a school of thought that believes that authentic people are loud. They reckon that you have to be noisy in order to be your authentic self. This category of people argues against authenticity because to them unless you are loud you may not be able to express your realness. Some of these people, who in some cases seem more on the quiet side, shy away from the discourse of authenticity. But these are issues of personality traits than it is of being authentic.

It is commonplace in any group discussion for instance, for assertive people to appear more visible, and easily steal the show because of their ease with communicating. What these people have is the ability to express themselves assertively, even when they are on the wrong side of a discourse. This assertiveness and authenticity is not exactly the same thing.

Our personalities differ, and that is perfectly okay. Loud does not necessarily mean authentic. It could be powered by fear and doubt. Quiet too does not necessarily translate to authentic. It could as well be powered by fear and doubt. Authenticity can be loud or quiet. It is simply being you. It is staying in the habitat of your make up.

Those who tend to speak against authentic people because they opined that authenticity makes one loud need to understand that authenticity in itself creates visibility by virtue of what it is. And not every one whose voice is the loudest in any group is being real.

Some do it to hide their struggles from complex. And for some other, it's just their personality. On the other hand, one can be quiet and still be very real. There is no right or wrong way for you to express who you are as long as you are not trying to be someone else.

So if you are an introvert, you don't have to conform to an extroverted nature before you are seen as being authentic. The originality of a genuine behaviour is mostly obvious, though never void of cynicism from some sect. This is very true in many cases because those who have left the comfort zone of conformity for self-actualization are rare.

Of course, such decision is not always an easy one. The point is no one should practice being another person. As long as you are being your real self in that capacity of your true nature, you are just as authentic as anyone else. And irrespective of your personality trait, confidently express your authenticity.

BEING YOUR AUTHENTIC SELF IS NOT ABOUT COMPARISONS

When people start comparing themselves to one another, then rots start to get into those gathering or relationship. Comparison is a very dangerous thing and it is common among insecure people. When you are sure and have fully accepted who you are, as uniquely made and suited for your own purpose, your only comparison would be with your vision, your purpose.

Comparing your talents, looks, gifts and possessions with someone else's is not wise and therefore something to be avoided completely. When the thoughts come, because they will come to your mind, it is important to resist it. There is usually no love where comparison exists. It breeds only envy and jealousy.

The world is large enough for all of us to succeed and thrive. The mind is the only limit you have if you refuse to grow it. And one major way to build up the mind is in reading. Paul of Tarsus, in describing what happens when people start comparing themselves to themselves, called it foolishness. In his words, "And they comparing themselves with themselves are foolish."

It is foolish because it shows you have deviated from your purpose and have disregarded the fact that God created you different from others. You are telling God that He should have done a "better" job at your creation.

Such line of thinking fails to acknowledge the peculiarity of each human being. In thinking like that you fail to see yourself as a beautiful and intelligent creature, placed on earth to get things done. Your focus has to be on your purpose, the things that make you more real. Find your unique self, refine it and stay there. This can never be over-emphasised.

Everyone was born a star but only a few shines because those are the ones who decided to have a tag on their star. When you are in your place of authenticity, you are perceived as a genius and that unveils your creativity; your genius will be perceived by others, and the world will come to you or hail your star. In other words, you become a star at what you were created specifically for, and the rest of humanity follows that light.

When you no longer have to analyze your life and possessions based on comparison with somebody else's; if you don't feel superior by thinking that you are the one who is better than every other person in the room and therefore deserves a preferential treatment; if you can confidently give a "no" to what you don't agree with or do not want to be part of without feeling sorry, then you know that you have truly accepted yourself. That, is an indication you are living your authentic life.

The whole idea of living your younique life is being comfortable with yourself and allowing the expression of who you truly are, regardless of what is being said or assumed about you.

People will always try to give you a narrative of how you ought to be, but you are the main character in the story of your life and if you refuse to play your lead role, the supporting actors will have to take your place, act it out and then direct you in the play called "you."

Unfortunately that becomes a problem. It's like giving out the power to the environment while you cry victim. This is your life and you ought to be in charge of it.

AUTHENTICITY IS NOT ABOUT BEING NICE AND NEVER SAYING NO TO PEOPLE

It is a good thing to be nice. Yes, it is humane to be nice actually but nice is not what I like to use in describing that attitude of sympathy towards others. I prefer to call that being good.

Being nice can be very costly. Nice won't allow you say a "no" to what you should not accept. It may not allow you to give people the opportunity to also learn from their own mistakes because you try being their "everything." That approach, in most cases, will wear you out.

Everybody deserves to enjoy the experience failure at some things brings. And you need to be good enough to let those who you love have that chance. They need to feel the pain you so nicely want to make them avoid. Through that, they will grow and build resilience.

When care is not taken, nice people tend go in the direction of people-pleasing without even noticing it. Being authentic does not suggest you become a "yes-yes" person. It does not suggest becoming everything to everyone at your detriment. As mentioned earlier, this approach can eventually tear you apart.

People, you must bear in mind, are never fully satisfied. There is the tendency to always want more from a source that is giving. Playing into their hands is not being authentic. Of course, a lot of people stay on it for fear of rejection or loneliness, but your primary obligation is to yourself, to maintain your sanity, and to make choices that do not deplete you of energy.

No matter how much you try to be everything to others, at some point in their lives, when you do finally give a "no" to some of their demands, even if it was just for once, all your previous "yeses" would have been forgotten and you will be labelled wrongly still. In the words of Barbara De Angelis, "We need to find the courage to say no to the things and people that are not serving us if we want to rediscover ourselves and live our lives with authenticity."

For me, that courage became an intentional quest. I have had to build the habit of saying no. I have had to counsel many people to do this too. It was not an easy thing to do. But through conscious and deliberate effort, I mastered the habit of giving a "no" to what I did not feel comfortable with.

The first thing you would notice when you start doing this will be the freedom it brings with it. And how I love that freedom! It took me some time before this happened but I am glad I made that decision at the time I did.

When you choose this path, you might experience criticisms and name-callings in the beginning. Some people may even think of you as having a bad attitude all because of your refusal to be manipulated. People thought of me in that way, because I wouldn't allow their emotional manipulation over me. But that did not bother me. My new-found freedom and sanity meant more to me.

What you may not know about people who never want a "no" from you is that in many instances, these same people may not accept to do for you the same things they make demand of from you. It's okay to do good for those who don't deserve it. In fact, they are the ones who really need it. However, showing acts of kindness does not mean that you lose control of how you distribute your resources and energy.

There is no authenticity in that. The goal should not be to be liked. It should be to be true to yourself. In the words of Joseph

Itiat, "You are not here, on this planet, to do the bidding of others. You are here, to find yourself, be yourself, and give of yourself within the parameters of your allotted abilities and convictions. Trying to impress everyone is a misplaced priority." In the long term, being your authentic self will serve you and others better. You will have more control of yourself and resources, and people will eventually understand how you want to be treated and engaged, and will have no other choice but to respect that.

It may not be an easy path to follow, but it is a worthy path to walk still. It's your life and you deserve to have absolute control. Bear in mind, the world is pretty loud out there with opinions on how and who you ought to be, but you are the one who owes yourself the commitment to stay true to yourself.

AUTHENTICITY IS NOT BEING INSENSITIVE TO THE FEELINGS OF OTHERS

Part of being authentic is appreciating diversity and different opinions because that is what happens when everyone is allowed to be themselves, without any fear of judgment or feeling of shame.

We are at our best when we are allowed to live and be just who we truly are. However, being yourself doesn't connote brashness or any form of lack of self-control under the guise of "that is just who I am."

Who you are is really great and no one is actually created by God to mess up other people. No one. We were made to have great positive multiplying effect on one another using our skills, talents, money and time. To hurt people under the pretence of "that is who I am" is an error and evidence of deficiency in emotional intelligence. Authentic people are empathetic and sympathetic.

People who are making tremendous world impacts are those who have found themselves, and are trying their best to help others do same. You cannot see yourself as the best with an eye of contempt towards others and still claim to be an authentic person.

No, that's not what authenticity is about. We were all created with and for good intentions. There is a high need for intentional sensitivity towards others, especially hurting and perceivably weak people. Your strength should be to their aid and not against them. Authentic people build others up, not tear them apart.

As an authentic person, you add value to other people. You do this through words of encouragement. You help them with your wealth or wisdom since God created every one of us for each other, to help in ways we can.

To put it simply, authenticity calls for empathy, sympathy and all that is good. The instant you are able to give of yourself, without having to change yourself or try to please anyone, without feeling compelled; the instant your decisions are naturally made, without unnecessary feeling of pressure to conform or play along, you are being authentic.

REFLECTIONS

In what ways will you learn to stay true to yourself without yielding to the pressure to compromise who you are?

_____

_____

_____

_____

_____

_____

_____

_____

_____

_____

_____

What are the things you would say do not constitute authenticity?

_____

_____

_____

_____

_____

_____

_____

_____

_____

_____

_____

05

BECOMING YOUNIQUE:
THE ROLE OF ADVERSITY AND SELF-AWARENESS

"Live authentically. Why would you continue to compromise something that's beautiful to create something that is fake?"
STEVE MARABOLI

I have been through a lot in my still very few years here on earth. People tell me that they consider me a very sympathetic soul. What they do not know is that I simply have become that. I sometimes go further to try and explain to them how I have turned out this way.

It turns out it was not something I read in a book. I actually wish I had read something which would have probably made my path an easy one to walk. That was not the case. The circumstances I found myself got me tutored into understanding how I am built.

I have experienced many delays in some things I thought I should have had and I have failed at so many opportunities. Adversity was one major leap to my inner growth. There were days I would pray for a way of escape. There were times I tried by every means to not go through what I went through, especially to make them go away.

What I fought turned out to build me up. Now I owe everything I have become to this process. I know what it means to not find that dream job and do jobs you feel more qualified for because you needed the money. I have known many pains. I can relate with people on different levels of grief, delay, and broken relationships.

When I write about coming out of adversity, or pain and maximizing them to discovering one's life and purpose, it is not theory. It is something I have been through. Not many people come out well as some would lose themselves to their troubles.

Nothing just happens in life. Even our troubles and those issues we think of as misfortunes, are all in the plan to help us find our purpose and live our lives as we should. In the words of Joseph Itiat, "The things you meet or encounter in the course of navigating within the sphere of human entities are all on errand to serve as your raw materials. What you do with them is entirely your call. If you let them shred you to pieces, that too, requires your permission."

On a personal note, I choose to use all that I go through as raw materials.

THE PLACE OF ADVERSITY

I do not think there is anything in life that has the power to turn us completely around than the way adversity does. It is like this: The pains and the troubles you go through can either make the best of you or the worst of you. But you will never remain the same after it.

Pain is a very loud teacher and an agonizing one at that. Pain cannot be compared to your most pleasured moments. However, if you can pay attention to it, the reasons it hurts and how it hurts, it could revolutionize your humanity forever.

For most people, adversity is a clue to their true younique life, a problem they were born to solve. In other words, where it hurts you the most might be your sign to what healing you are to bring to the word.

As would be agreed by many, our adversities humble us. If not for anything, it makes us come to terms with ourselves. Yes, it has a way of bringing us back to where we should have begun in the first place. And in the process of it all, we discover our abilities and inabilities; our strengths and weaknesses; our skills and talents. To put it simply, we get to know who we are.

This discovery is due to the fact that we had to make use of them for a way of escape! When you are beaten and in need of help, your mind is working really hard to find help out of the situation. And in that process, you find out who you are, and some strengths you didn't even know you possessed. You realize that you are stronger than what has been holding you down.

That humbling effect our troubles have on us is a major breakthrough on character moulding. I would never have been able to bear up to people and difficult circumstances with faith were it not for the troubles I had been through. In agreement with Coco Chanel, "Hard times arouse an instinctive desire for authenticity."

The things we go through and the victory we experience has a way of building up our faith. It has a way of serving as a reference point to the possibility of emerging victorious in the midst of oppression. Series of such victory can toughens one up for impending challenges. They become valid testimonies and the bedrock of strength needed for life.

Struggling with shyness and low self-esteem, I could not do a lot. I was hindered. Not by anything external, but by myself. For a long time, this hindered my progress in many areas. I had a message but could not pass it across. I didn't have the confidence to do it. It was a huge challenge.

That was not unique to me. I was in great company because

great be the company of those who are faced with different challenges. It may not look so to you until you speak to even the people you admire from afar. The point is every one of us has challenges. It is what keeps our humanity in check.

Challenges are not to our despair. Of course, it never looks that way, hence no one prays for it. Everyone seems to pray against it. However, challenges are part of the fabric of our existence so that we can learn, and discover what we are capable of. If you will allow your adversity the opportunities it offers for your growth, you will be amazed at what you can become.

The underlying principle in adversity is same as with the growth of trees in the desert and those from a normal soil. You cannot compare trees that grow up in the desert to those by a normal pasture ground close to water source. Those trees in the desert, by reason of their struggle for water, stretch roots down to the nearest river they can reach. This could be hundreds of miles apart sometimes. By this way, their growth is radically tough and not easily destroyed, making them last for decades and some for centuries.

It is the same with challenges. You grow inner strength by reason of the battles you have had to overcome. You develop character this way. Of course, no one really finds trouble palatable and they are not moments we wish for. But if you hold on and allow the lessons learned during the time of distress guide you, it will not only transform you, it will change you for good and also transform the life of anyone that will ever meet with you.

The call to living your younique life does not displace the possibility of dealing with adversity. But even in the face of adversity, you can turn that into something that is of service to you. No one remains the same after going through adversity, but the nature of what we all become is dependent on what we choose to make of what we have gone through.

The experience of adversity changes people. No one stays the same. You start to see things from different angles. If you were never sympathetic, and you were schooled to be so through adversity, you genuinely become so.

If your life had been void of empathy, and the rocky path life throws you on, schooled you to learn empathy, you genuinely expressed that because you have known pain; it becomes easier for you to empathize with others going through challenges in their lives too.

We are all inexcusable as far as the call to leading our younique lives is concerned. No matter our experiences, we can learn, deploy and maintain the right attitude during this time, and allow ourselves to go through the process of being refined, and made better.

This is quite important because we are surrounded by many people who gave in to their troubles. These have lost their voices, and have concluded they cannot amount to much.
You should not end up that way no matter what happens. You must join the crew of those who believe that they are stronger than whatever they may be facing in life. In other words, see adversity as designed to bring out the part of you that is golden.

It is true that adversity can lead to bitterness. But when people allow bitterness into their lives because they thought they didn't deserve their sufferings, they come out worse off.

Of course, pain can be terrible, but in the embrace of pain we transcend its power, leading only to the acquisition of lessons. Consequently, we become schooled voices, an encouragement and inspiration to other people who will go through similar situations. That way, we make a difference with our lives in spite of where we have been. That way, we lose not our authenticity, but use our all for the general good of humanity.

What this means is this: You can find yourself, find your path, and maximize your abilities even in trying periods. In other words, adversity is not the time to wallow in pity and how unfortunate you think you are. It is the time to build up your muscles and inner strength while becoming your real self in the process. Adversity will reveal who you are and that revelation will serve as a tool with which you gain clarity of your purpose and what it is you should be doing.

THE PLACE OF SELF-AWARENESS

Self-awareness is a conscious knowledge of your own character and feelings. It is actually being aware and acquainted with Self. According to Wikipedia, "Self-awareness is the capacity for introspection and the ability to recognize oneself as an individual separate from the environment and other individuals." Self-awareness then depends on an understanding of your past and present self.

No one can really say for sure what exactly the future is, although some tools are there for some expert predictions on some matters. But this is still not an absolute. Being aware of Self can go a long way to change the direction of your life especially if you have had a past you are not so proud of.

If you can carry out an honest evaluation of yourself, what you have been through, your reactions and responses to what you went through and compare that to your current self and situations, you can by this simple exercise, transform the projectile of your life's direction forever! But the key is to be honest with self and become more aware of your thoughts, your experiences with people and the influence of the environments you have lived in.

To become more aware of Self, you have to reflect a lot on your life and also become more aware of your thoughts. What is it you think about most? Ask questions about you and get intimated with reasons you do certain things. What makes you respond differently to some things and in some way to some people? What do you think makes you different? And why do you reckon that some things have happened in some ways that seem peculiar to only you?

This is a call to the study of yourself. And that is a good thing. Not a lot of people do this. Many of us would boast of how well we know of someone else while we are rarely aware of who we are. Those who want to live according to what they are designed for must pay attention to the proclivities of their heart. You ought to be the first thing to be known by you.

There may be blind spots here and there, but that should not be a reason to be ignorant of yourself. This habit of becoming more aware of self may seem unpleasant at first especially if it is something you have not really been engaged in before now. But as with other things in life, you will master it with more practice. The most important part is to start.

Begin with an internal self-talk. Relate with you. For me, it wasn't really a nice experience initially. By the time I began to reflect on my actions and inactions, I saw some parts of me that were not so pleasant. Sometimes I would get defensive, but over time, I had to tell myself the truth by giving myself an honest feedback and receiving same from others, so I could grow thereby.

Everyone needs this spiritual practice.

Self-awareness makes for the judgment of oneself by oneself so that one does not get judged by another. It is the sort of examination where the examiner and the student are one and the same. The seriousness of the call to lead an authentic life requires that every soul in pursuit of the mastery of self, and the deployment of self, in authentic measure, does this.

If you can learn about someone else and be so good at it that they become almost predictable to you, then you should expend greater energy on knowing who you truly are. Becoming your authentic self is one great impact that self-awareness helps you achieve. When you become aware of who you truly are, you can give expression and direction to it. You cannot claim to lead an authentic life without first being aware of yourself.

It is pertinent that you know from here that your authentic self is an evolving process but it is already who you are. It only requires your confidence to accept it and allow it freedom to be expressed from your heart. All of us are ever evolving until we finally leave this earth. You cannot fully know Self yet, that's why you are sometimes surprised by the things you do? We mostly are!

The next important exercise to do is to start a "detoxification" process of Self. By this, I mean that you unlearn some things you had believed up until this moment about yourself, especially very limiting and disempowering ways of life that has caused so much limitation and chaos in your life.

It is your responsibility to get rid of those chaotic ways that are in disharmony with your authentic self. This you have to do, then relearn again and continue learning until you are becoming the 'you' of your dreams. Everyone committed to creating the future they want, are committed to the practice that empowers for such creation.

While this may not be easy, make the decision to transform your life to the person you have seen yourself become and then be ready to face the loads of criticism that will come at you.

Criticism will come because the decision to be authentic and be your younique self will rarely be easily acceptable by the familiar folks in the environment around you. You should not be surprised if the people that are unwelcoming of the new you be members of your family and circle of friends. The truth is to lead the life you are built for, you must be ready to go through anything.

You must also spend time with yourself for the sole purpose of knowing yourself intimately. That ruggedness, in the face of adversity, and the commitment to knowing yourself, will take you to a fuller knowledge of who you are and what you are built for. Be deliberate therefore, and become more present with your thoughts and your presence.

REFLECTIONS

How will you become more aware of yourself from today?

_____

_____

_____

_____

_____

_____

In what area of your life do you need more self-acceptance?

_____

_____

_____

_____

_____

How well do you think you have loved self, if not well, how do you plan to work on that aspect of your life?

_____

_____

_____

_____

_____

What will you start doing from today in order to become more aware of self?

_____

_____

_____

_____

_____

_____

EVOLVING INTO YOUR YOUNIQUE SELF

"To love yourself right now, just as you are, is to give yourself heaven. Don't wait until you die. If you wait, you die now. If you love, you live now."
ALAN COHEN

The fear of "what will people say about me?" has crippled more lives to a mediocre status than any other flaw they think they might have. If because of some fears you become laid back with your life, or refuse to take daring steps and risks, what you do not know is that you will have more regrets later.

It is one thing to get your identity on and another one entirely to begin expressing who you are confidently. Having suffered self-hate myself, another major work I had to do was self-love.

I had been self-battered with self-hate and low self-esteem. Everything was becoming too difficult. I needed to reverse things. Interestingly, it is often said that life has no vacuum. In other words, to delete one thought, you must replace it with another.

As I embarked on the journey of being myself and truly living my life's purpose, I began to see that opposition could arise from expressing myself. We are rarely prepared for all that life can throw our way!

The most disappointing part of this reality is the opposition that might come from those who are closest to you. While that is so, you have to know that it is all part of the deal.

Fear of other people's opinions and what the world thinks of you can threaten to cripple all your efforts at being real. Allowed, it can make a mess of your younique life. However, you must remember that unless you give voice to the meaning of your life, no one else will.

You have to make your demands of life. Nothing extra-ordinary is given for free. That's why you have to fight to be your authentic self, regardless of what others think of you. That way, you can become significant. In other words, you cannot afford to live a barely-get-by life.

Becoming your authentic self is not trying to achieve perfection. It is accepting yourself and being grateful for what, and who you are. Perfection is what we are always afraid of, or course. We fear being judged as perfect if we express ourselves so confidently. Against this backdrop, we would rather pretend to be like everyone else than make unique moves, expressing our difference.

Being yourself does not mean you have to be perfect or that you are perfect. And if anyone judges you so, then good for you! You shouldn't hold back for just any reason or any person, that's my point. There is never a justification for holding back.

Being the real you is important for you to live out your life's purpose. That's the call everyone must answer. Until you accept who you are and decide to be original, your journey to fulfilling purpose can become really difficult.

Everyone has their life to live and a mark to make in the area of their calling. Being your younique self is the easiest way you can go about achieving that purpose without so much burden. Among other factors, there are three that can be of help in the journey towards actualizing your authenticity.

ACCEPT WHO YOU ARE

In my journey to living my younique life so far, especially in the area of inter-personal relationship with those who are trying to also figure themselves out, there is nothing that I have found truer than the fact that most people quietly loathe themselves or something about themselves.

Sometimes the root problem lies in the difficulty they have in accepting their family backgrounds, their past, and maybe their looks. Many people just wish for some ridiculous things. Some who are royalty wish to have a different life while those who have a different life from royalty wish to live in royalty, and in some cases, gets depressed for not experiencing royalty.

Don't let what you have no control over begin to control your life. That's signing up for a frustrated life. The truth is, at the root of some drug abuse cases, low self-esteem issues, body shaming, poor self-image, trust issues, depression and even suicides, is a lack of self-acceptance. According to Wikipedia, "Self-acceptance is an individual's satisfaction or happiness with oneself, and is thought to be necessary for good mental health." The absence of good mental health is a bane to the development of self-actualization. It can affect the fulfilment of your purpose.

Self-awareness helps with self-acceptance and a firm stand on one's identity of Self. What it does is make you aware of Self so you can get acquainted with your being. For instance, in becoming more aware of yourself, you may find out reasons you have difficulty in relating with other people. While you may realize your flaws and weaknesses, you should take note of your many good nature too because the human mind tends more towards the negative than it does the positive. You are not all bad. No one is. You have a good soul regardless of how it's been with you.

The next thing to do, having assessed yourself and realized you still have a lot to work on in terms of improving the areas you aren't so proud of, is to accept that this is how you are now. That is what self-acceptance simply means. It is accepting who and how you are at the time.

Accepting who you are now is what will aid you to become who you ought to be faster. You have to accept the family you are born into and appreciate the life you have been given. Accept that although there are some things you will have to improve on, you also have a lot to congratulate yourself for and be grateful for too. You have to accept your looks, height, and body size. You have to accept the sound of your voice, texture of your hair, your race and your skin colour. To put it simply, just accept yourself as you are, and if you know that you have fitness issues, work on being fit.

Everyone has things to deal with. We all have "thorns" we've all got to deal with. Whatever it is, what we need to do is first of all accept who we are now and at the moment. That is the foundation for authentic living and the bedrock for building our confidence because it helps improve our self-image.

The introvert for instance, who wishes to be more engaging with others should first of all accept that being an introvert is not a deficiency. That way, the decision to be more engaging will not become a burden to lose one's originality. It's great to want to work on one's social skills, but we should not try to change who we are at the core.

People who have accepted themselves are confident people. They are not proud. That is because they understand their fallibility and tend to humbly accept that there is no perfection with people. They tend to believe that since they are not without struggles, others are not as well.

As a result of this thinking, they do not expect perfection from others, and tend to be very sympathetic and empathetic with other peoples' struggles because they know how that feels, having had to deal with many of life's struggles too. They also tend to be less judgmental and less critical of others.

There is a lot that hinges on accepting yourself. Even loving others as you ought to, depends on how well you have accepted yourself. It can be difficult to love others if you haven't experienced an acceptance of yourself.

I mean, how do you really claim to accept another and love them when you loath you? It is the one of the reasons some people treat others so badly. Because they haven't learnt to give themselves that humanly regard, they become unable to give what they do not give themselves. People who hate themselves cannot show love to others. They end up hurting themselves and other people.

Truly healthy relationships of any kind are expressed by people who already love themselves and so adorn others with the outpour of that love.

Self-acceptance is not being selfish. It is the fundamental requirement for the fulfilment of treating others as you would love to be treated. Vironika Tugaleva nailed it perfectly when she said, "I only accept your mistakes and flaws to the degree that I accept my own."

FORGIVE YOURSELF

One of the things that hold people back from expressing their authentic selves is the feeling of guilt. Guilt can produce a feeling of shame and fear and can make it even difficult to connect with your true self. It does interfere with one's ability to be creative, and can limit your expression of all the beautiful things you can offer this world. Self-guilt can make you feel awful by always bringing up all the things that should really be in your past.

To make real progress in terms of being yourself, you have to forgive yourself for whatever you may have done. Everyone needs to do this if they must move on with their life and create the life they are built for. You must put the past behind you for good. That is not negotiable.

The truth is, none of us is really perfect and so the standards we set for ourselves and others can be mere fantasy. There is no need to be hard on ourselves. Sadly, some of us would accept that God forgives. We even asked for forgiveness from others and accepted it when they forgave us. But when it comes to ourselves, we find it hard to forgive ourselves. We deal ourselves harder blow. Nothing great can come out of that.

One of the ways of overcoming the hold of something done in the past is in sharing it with someone whose loyalty you can count on. When shared, one can feel better and grow above the grip of such hold. The truth is, whatever happened in the past should be left there. Today offers a new chance to do better, be better and make progress.

While one may not be proud of what took place in the past, the past should not place limitation on the extent you can make progress. As long as one is still on a journey to making things right, the past should be left there. Life is a process. Allow it.

Becoming your authentic self is letting go of any projection that does not align with who you are at the core. It is becoming comfortable with who you are. This step up can help with the feeling of loneliness, because in being your authentic self, you accept, love and be-friend self.

Truly authentic people can be loving and fun to be with. I am not saying that you become perfect once you are authentic. No, far from that. But you truly learn to be sympathetic towards other people because of the awareness of what it takes for any significant change to occur in a person's life.

The key thing to note is this: Your real self is nothing to be ashamed of. You owe no one an explanation class for your life's stories. There is absolutely no reason of being ashamed of where you are coming from. Truth is, almost everyone has a past they are not proud of. And most of our learning comes from where we have been.

Self-shaming can arise from not forgiving yourself. It can cause you to seek validation from others because of the feeling of not being capable of being much. Where care is not taken, you could turn yourself into a slave of other peoples' opinion. It can even lead to hypocritical behaviour, making you pretend to be who you are not for fear of being judged.

Such way of living can keep you locked down and cause you to lead a life of inferiority. Fully acknowledge that you can lead an authentic life. Take pride in who you are. However, do not deny that you need to grow in some areas too. To put it simply, forgive yourself and create the life you desire.

LOVE YOURSELF

In one of His admonitions, Jesus Christ of Nazareth said, "Love your neighbour as you love yourself." It turns out a lot of us only stick with a part of this commandment. There are those who love themselves and do not care about others. There are those who care about others but do not pay attention to themselves. We seem to not pay attention to the commandment holistically.

We are admonished to love ourselves. But the decisions we make most times betray this. In relationships, we often stick with people we should have let out of our lives, for instance. These people, though harmful to us, are given space in our life. We ignore our sanity and stay in relationships that are leading to dead ends. In such cases, we simply do not love ourselves enough.

Part of self-love is learning to let go of things and of people that only occupy space but do not add value to us. It is learning to let go of people who only take from us but do not give back.

Self-love requires having a sense of value for yourself. It requires seeing yourself through a lens of confidence and high worth, such that you do not get to depend on validation from others. This is not dismissing the need for feedback.

Feedback is great as long as it comes out of concern and constructive criticism. Self-loving people seek for feedback. Not validation. There is a difference. The key thing is to love yourself to the point you are not at the mercy of what people say or think of you.

In the practice of self-love, you take yourself to places that have the potency of contributing to your growth. This practice opens you up to making new friends, meeting new people, and gives you the chance to build useful networks. Consequently, you can collaborate as a result of this and start new projects or build on past ones.

You never get to give yourself these opportunities if you do not think you are deserving of much, if you do not love yourself. Everyone gets an opportunity to live a new life at every dawn of a new day. It is believe in oneself, a direct product of self-love that makes for seamlessly taking advantage of the opportunities that abound in each day.

It takes self-love to place great value on your personality, appreciate what you are becoming and what great job God did at creating you. Living this way is not difficult at all. I did not say it is easy. But everyone can start at the place of gratitude and appreciation for life. If you are struggling with loving yourself, or viewing yourself from the right lens, start first with gratitude and appreciation for the life you have. See the future you want to create and be thankful and grateful for that person you are about to become.

Such little act is powerful enough to change your self-perception, and open you up for embracing opportunities. Staying on this track increases your sense of self-value, and will directly affect how you truly love other people. When you have actually learnt to be in love with yourself, it builds up your confidence, removes shameful feelings from your life and then makes it easier for you to be yourself.

It is really difficult to claim that you are living your true life if you do not love yourself. Again, even this, begins at the place of accepting yourself. It extends to the need to forgive yourself for what you may have done to yourself and maybe to others too.

Self-love encompasses every good deed. In practicing it, self-acceptance is required. To put it simply, self-love promotes originality, authenticity. This process, of becoming you, is your story; it is the journey you can share with the world so others can learn from. I have had to deal with a lot of struggles. But I have refused to let that limit me. I choose to create with my struggles.

Everyone can do so because everyone has a story. Living your younique life is a key to knowing and exuding peace. Loving yourself is the gateway to this inner peace. Failing in this area will make it look as though the world is at war with you. Succeeding at this will translate to inner peace, and that will give birth to outer peace. There is no greater attainment.

REFLECTIONS

What must you do for yourself in order to live your younique life?

_____

_____

_____

_____

_____

_____

_____

_____

When will you start doing those answers in the last question above?

_____

_____

_____

_____

_____

_____

_____

_____

What will you have to let go so as to live the life that you want?

_____

_____

_____

_____

_____

_____

_____

LIVE YOUR YOUNIQUE LIFE

"We have to dare to be ourselves, however frightening or strange that self may prove to be."
MAY SARTON

You can live your younique life. The world is a crowded place, with so much talents, gifts and great people. If you do not identify with who you are, you may just add you up to the generalities.

You do not need to be part of that statistics. You are more than some population statistics. You are a very younique soul. But until you realize it and believe strongly in that, you may just live as one of the billions of people on the planet who are just occupying space.

What is easy is to condemn oneself and consider oneself as being unworthy. Anyone can do that. Some have been consistent in such way of living, to the point they cannot look someone else in the eye without panicking in their thoughts.

Ever been in a situation where you had prepared for the stage only to come for the show and see the calibre of people out there waiting for you and fear suddenly grips you? One of the reasons this happens is because of deficiency in great belief in oneself.

We sometimes think of ourselves as too little and are even ashamed, sometimes, of who we are. This is different from being nervous. Nervousness is okay. I am talking about seeing yourself as low and shying away from the life you should create.

There is no justification for sentencing yourself to a life of mediocrity. You are a product of God and do not deserve to lead a laid back life. The call is that you get up, get out, and live the life you have been wired for. In the words of Joseph Itiat, "Your greatest obligation to yourself and the sphere of human existence is the alignment of your navigation within the earth school to how and for what you are wired."

In my personal experience so far with people, I have realized that most people judge themselves as too small, and not worth a lot. They see themselves as "grasshoppers", compare to others. Whereas these people may not think little of them, they conclude they are thought of as nothing.

We mostly tend to think less of ourselves because of our struggles. For some of us, we are so afraid we cannot look others in the eye. We tend to think that if we do, they will see through us. In an effort to hide these things, we look down on ourselves and relegate ourselves to the back seat.

Everybody has a struggle. There is rarely a person without issues they wouldn't want to let out. The people you see and think have it all are themselves not without struggles. But you see the difference between those that are up there, creating the life they want and those that are down here, hosting pity party is this: One group believes they are capable of more. The other group thinks they are capable of less.

Your job is to remove any doubt you may have about yourself. Your job is to free up yourself so the world can make room for you. No one stands in the way of the one with clarity of destination. The power lies within you to unlock what it is the world has not been able to perceive about you.

You have to give yourself a chance before you can get the audience of other people. This requires boldness and courage, and rightly so.

It takes boldness and courage to be your true self. It takes that to fulfil your purpose. Sadly, everyone would love to be great, but few are willing to do what greatness demands.

There is no guarantee you won't experience setbacks. If there is a certainty in the pursuit of authentic living, it is that you will face challenges. I am yet to meet a great person who has not dealt with setbacks.

I have seen wonderful people who have been rejected severally at almost everything they had done yet they still kept trying, never giving up. Jack MA of Alibaba, a great admiration to me, has had to start over and over again despite his past records of rejections.

What is appealing to the world today, in his case is his success story. Like Jack MA and others like him, you will have to walk the path of resilience. This applies to everyone who desires to walk the path of authenticity.

Living your younique life is not without huge demands. You may be rejected, but rejection for you should not be an obstacle. It should spur you to dare more, to be more and to attain greatness.

Your authenticity should not be traded for anything at all. It is the only foundation to build on. It is the right way to start. You need your originality to make your achievements long lasting and firmly rooted. Like a house, if it must stand the test of time, it must be built on the right foundation.

Your real self is like the blueprint of a house. It is a finished work within you. Your job is to birth it. Your duty is to align your daily choices to how you are wired. It is there in your feelings, attitudes and in all things that make you. It's in your heart. You just need to live it out.

You should not let fear stop you. Freely recognize your fears, and feel free to be nervous at times, but stay in motion. Know that you are capable. This knowing will get you going. When the curtains are drawn, and you are out there, you will just do it.

That's the attitude you must have as one who is committed to living your younique life. Do not allow anything to limit your advancement, your commitment to authenticity. Embrace every challenge with the will to create stories out of them, to create victories in spite of them.

Do not give others the room to determine how far you can go. Allow the lives of the people who need your message and mental massage to spur you on. Again and again you must tell yourself that you are capable of living your younique life. That is the reason it is laid in your heart. Let that be your motivation. It will push you towards doing what needs to be done for the sake of humanity.

Above all else, choose to be yourself. It will make it easier to deal with all other things and you would be better and live better. With such commitment, purpose becomes clearer and your networks, better. You have no business being someone else. You are the best interpretation of your life and that cannot be taken away from you. It is less costly to be real than it is faking other people's lifestyles. Please always remember that. Make the commitment to become aware of yourself and live the life you were born for. That's when we get to celebrate you, maybe not immediately, but eventually! Let the will to live your younique life not be relinquished to anyone but you. In the words of Niccolo Machiavelli, "Where the willingness is great, the difficulties cannot be great."

REFLECTIONS

How do you think you have been living your younique life?

_____

_____

_____

_____

_____

_____

What will you stop doing henceforth to truly be your younique self?

_____

_____

_____

_____

_____

_____

Write down what habits you will start to master henceforth in order for you to live your younique life?

_____

_____

_____

_____

_____

_____

What one thing has this book done for you that could help in fulfilling your purpose?

_____

_____

_____

_____

_____

Congratulations!

That you have read this book up to this point is proof of your interest in living your younique life. And that is really great. It is decisions such as this that can determine your destiny.

I'm not going to make it long here. I only want to remind you of a few things.

Firstly, henceforth become more aware of your presence.

Secondly, don't live anyhow.

Thirdly, if like me, you were born into deep rooted beliefs of different cultural norms, your fight of faith as we have discussed in this book might be tougher, coming from that background. My sincere advice to you therefore is this: Become more intentional.

Yes, be deliberate in assessing all the popular stuff you heard has always been the way to do many things. They may have been passed down by your parents or people you respect. But you are not their thinking.

This is your own life. This is your own time. Regardless of who your mentor was, is, or will be, your say matters.

You are too special and so youniquely made. Hence, you cannot live anyhow or just make choices as the people you see.

Be deliberate and intentional in everything you do. Be deliberate in choosing what you believe, who you spend most of your time with and how you make use of your time. Be intentional in everything you choose to do. Be it starting a business, getting married, or having children.

Start business intentionally. Marry intentionally. Have children and raise them intentionally. Do nothing because of cultural demands. Do everything because you are ready, and well prepared to do so. Doing otherwise, either for selfish reasons or due to ignorance or negligence might lead to making your life or that of another person miserable.

It is true that we cannot control everything around us. But do not, because of that belief, lose control of the things you should have control over. Let purpose drive your decisions.

And above everything else, believe in God. Let your belief in God and His love for humanity translate towards others in the way that you treat them. Let it show in the excellence you display in doing your work or in producing genuine products for your customers as a business person. Let your way of life be evidence that you know God.

This is not a call to perfection as you will definitely get it wrong sometimes. But let your wrongs be errors due to your fallibility as a human soul. Let it not be an intentional design to hurt another younique soul. If anyone would be doing such act, let it not be you.

Live intentionally. Be authentic. Be driven by purpose.

Live your younique life.

Your Friend,

Joy Iseki

I WOULD LIKE US TO
CONTINUE THIS CONVERSATION

REACH ME VIA EMAIL
isekijoy@gmail.com

FOLLOW MY BLOG
https://www.joyiseki.com/blog

FOLLOW ME ON
INSTAGRAM @joyiseki :: TWITTER @isekijoy
FACEBOOK facebook.com/joyiseki

JOIN OUR NEW
FACEBOOK COMMUNITY GROUP AND PAGE
https://www.facebook.com/groups/theyouniquemindscommunity
http://fb.me/liveyouryouniquelife

THANK YOU!

ACKNOWLEDGEMENT

To my friend, mentor and teacher, Joseph ITIAT, I thank you. Your direct and timely suggestions made this work turn out differently.

To my long time friend, Mr Solomon Pereemiwee BATIFE, a very big thank you. You encouraged me at first to put this piece together.

ABOUT THE AUTHOR

A Cognitive and Behavioural Therapist, Joy Iseki is passionate about helping people live their authentic lives. She uses several medium to promote the concept of embracing one's uniqueness so purpose can be fulfilled. Presently the CEO, Kharitoos Plus, she lives in Lagos, Nigeria.

Printed in Great
Britain
by Amazon